Isaiah 62:6

I have set watchmen upon thy walls, O Jerusalem, which shall never hold their peace day nor night: ye that make mention of the LORD, keep not silence

I have never been diligent to scripture, nor have I been a part of chosen dogma. I was raised as a Catholic, but have departed that faith.

Luke 21:12-18

[12] *But before all these, they shall lay their hands on you, and persecute you, delivering you up to the synagogues, and into prisons, being brought before kings and rulers for my name's sake.*

[13] *And it shall turn to you for a testimony.*

[14] *Settle it therefore in your hearts, not to meditate before what ye shall answer:*

[15] *For I will give you a mouth and wisdom, which all your adversaries shall not be able to gainsay nor resist.*

[16] *And ye shall be betrayed both by parents, and brethren, and kinsfolk, and friends; and some of you shall they cause to be put to death.*

[17] *And ye shall be hated of all men for my name's sake.*

[18] *But there shall not an hair of your head perish.*

Before I knew my salvation I was a great and mighty sinner. I lacked a humble nature as I lived in the sin of pride, so much that the living almost killed me. No man or woman could separate me from my own hubris. It was only in the love of Light in the

1

Living God in which I came to know my vocation as a writer.

He has given me a partner and guiding friends. And so I live at the disposal of Our Almighty God to glorify the vast blessings of his son Jesus Christ fearlessly scribing the promises of his only begotten son, so that we as a nation may once again claim justice for Life, Liberty and the Pursuit of Happiness.

Praise the Almighty Father

Watchman on the Gate

by Martin H. Petry

Preface

It may be helpful to the reader to know that this work is an evolution based upon another writing known as *Hypocronance*.

Another book I co-authored with Tracy LeCates known as *Convoking Hell* might also be helpful for the reader interested in qualifying my authority to make the claims in the following pages.

A reader of this work may also gain benefit for visiting our webpage www.usamutt.com The links I provide in the pages that follow will all be accessible in a dedicated category know as Watchman Links.

I apologize for the unusual format of this piece in advance, but all the links give a frame of mind reference to the words I have written while introducing the links.

While we consider the future of our country and the upcoming elections we must dismiss the apathy we all own in speaking to our collective troubles of the day.

We must deny the nitwittery that dismisses truths of our founding father's motivations. The truth of separation of Church and State has been hijacked. The Constitution doesn't say that church and state are separate; it says that the state will not proclaim one religion over another. Our truth as a country is that we found our freedoms and Bill of Rights as they were given to us by God, or a Creator, not from man.

My contention is a simple one; we suffer as a country because we have forgotten the responsibility of maintaining our inalienable rights. Political Correctness has become a fad that endures the chaos, which result's in giving power to a governance of tyranny. We were born in sin and for that sin we know choice. We cannot blame God for that which we have designed ourselves; we can realize our forgetting or turning our backs to the Almighty for the sake of our own convenient vices and retain the reward for such doings, or we can embrace the blessings of returning to wisdom within the promises of The Living God Jesus Christ.

Men's promises mean nothing as is evident for the last general and midterm elections. Watchman on the Gate is an unusual bit of writing for these very unusual days of living. What the reader must decide is what choice can be made for restoring our greatness as a nation. I am here to point out where the greatness comes from and lives.

June 24, 2010

I have been informed that for one reason unknown to me that a chronicle was to be written of events that lead us to this day and the results of this undoing. Our country, these United States of America was founded on the principles of Judeo Christian thinking and today President Obama along with Progressive Socialists are undoing the fabric of our Country's design.

Here is a link to a You Tube I just watched; http://www.youtube.com/watch?v=tPtaMgqOwL4

A book I wrote previously, which describes the dynamic I coined as *Hypocronance* offers a discussion of our immediate past as well as our past decades. It speaks to America as wanting a Utopia. It speaks to those who know better in managing a country as having turned their backs from rugged individualism. It speaks to being more interested in one's own condition as some type of manner to become more equal.

I have been drawn to studying scripture in this past week. It is no accident, either.

Many of us have turned away from our faith and belief. Many of us are helpless and hopeless. But some of us - a minority - are not forgetful of our principles. We are not guided by the measures of a progressive definition as to what is determined as fair. We know that life isn't fair. We know that because of our own apathy, fairness of life has become a nightmare of insanity.

Definitions and traditions we hold dearly are eroding away. For the first time in our Country's history, our next generation has less than the last. Moreover, it is criminally unprepared for what life will require of them so as to maintain our loved Standard of Living.

We became lazy and unguarded. We threw in with those who hate and denounce rugged individualism and believed in a kinder, better way of life. That folly of hypocronance is the burden of our future. And that burden is a mighty bit of needed fixes.

June 29, 2010

Recently I took council with Pastor Paol. He and his family visited us here at Staven Rescue. I asked him of supporting Israel in the realm of politics because it gave me great concerns. While we as a country have always been allies of those living under the Star of David, we are now a country that has changed our thinking through a President.

His answer was plainly simple and even as I heard it before, I never heard it with similar understanding. Our love and support for Israel is truly important, but we are never to support violence or evil intentions of any men. We spoke more from this vain as we arrived at an answer that Christians, Muslims and Jews all come from the God of Abraham. Because we have put our understanding of whom and what that God of Abraham is, we have difference of opinion.

Moses instructed us to live within ten laws. Since then The Son of Man came to reclaim authority as the teacher. His lesson made living in God's favor even more simplified as he instructed in following that path to God's Favor by two rules. Jesus came as a Jew and through the Holy Ghost became a Christian.

The very contention of dysfunction today is due to a belief of Jesus as the Messiah, or savior of men. That single aspect, the question of faith is Man's inescapable burden regardless of ritual or offering of faith.

As a man Jesus preached to men, he preached to those who claimed to live by God's law even better than they could and for his teachings; his authority as the Son and King of men was the very reason for his death. Those who could hear his words never gained for hearing them. Many even perished for speaking to their faith. Those who heard his words but denied faith in him as the King of men were those who delivered his peril to those who did believe in him, and it still goes on.

Jesus retold us of God's will. He reminded us of God's love for us. He even made God's will more understandable and then he told us all of what was to come. And still we forget ourselves even with evidence abundant of a truth. I know many who live without any faith in the Word of God. I know others who value a particular faith of belief who don't live by the Divine Trinity. There are also those claiming to know a particular version of what Jesus taught us. Many remain clueless as to God's will, even for hearing the words.

Time has come for me to know things I don't want to know.

Being a man of irreverent manners and arrogance I've come to realize my greatest sin is pride. That being said, I am humbled and broken. The fall of my pride has left me hearing the words of faithfulness, which led me to a place of spiritual desolation I need to live in, rather than speak to all of my wisdom.

If I don't move towards that example I have of Man's Savior and his teaching, I will remain as Hell's Vengeance is released upon the world, unsaved in rapture.

The dread in my heart confounds me as I hold this wisdom and see the world unfold upon itself just as the angels of the Lamb are released in the opening of the seven seals.

My heart's fury knows the tempo of the tribes arguing their own wisdom, while forgetting the Promise of the Son of Man. I keep with the arrogance of prideful thinking not knowing any Kingdom here on earth. I have no possessions to count against influence of these days, so the ranting of my contemplations receiving wealth here on earth are nothing more than lost in the deafening argument the tribes' banter.

So, the dilemma, as I reckon it is this; in the 46 years of my life we as a country have come to a haughtiness of unacceptable identity. What we were known for has been said to be an evolution, but it isn't. We may have great wisdom for our designs, but we lack any faith as a people considering the Son of Man's teachings. Our edginess for science is awe-inspiring. Books have been written by surgeons of such expert procedures, demonstrating God Complexes. Structures have been built no ancient engineers could have imagined, and we have become self important.

Those who have faith go unheard while those who know the words and deny the meaning act as deities and live like monarchs. And then we have those who tickle the spirit of light; they make claim for their earthly gain as evidence of their righteousness and pave the path to Hell. And I bear witness to it, just as the oil flows in the Gulf of Mexico today. For all of this: We witness the prophecies of the Lamb and every *problem child issue* grows in import.

The Lord said he would come as a thief in the night, and I say to you that there is no need to be such a thief. The chaos that abounds now is surely insane.

We maintain a presumption of morality that is based on lofty greed and love of evil design; all while we hold ourselves mighty for example of our hubris. Example of the felling amasses and no witness will bear testimony to the incarnate destructive tendency. They will distract, they will pontificate and they will opine the birth of their own lechery and say, "See how good we are, feel the worship of our needy idolatry, and embrace the love," all while spitting on Jesus, the Son of MAN.

Maybe my promised greatness isn't virtue. I am a man of contemplations and flavor, but maybe my greatness is as it as always has been. Maybe it is my calling to see all for what it is and then bear testimony to it. That remains unknown to me. Then again, maybe I will wake up and realize I am full of shit and get to the work that needs doing. There are great numerations of those who will bear testimony to that fact. You see, I am a man of my word, even if the promise I made was not forthright in delivery for the compensation.

I could stay where I am…. I can take whatever I want and dream of glory like no other. I CAN do such, but my curiosity has led me to a fork in the road. At this place all I know is right in front of me, and all I have left behind lurks in shadows I need to step through.

I wrote of desperate times on a trek through the wilderness of the Everglades, and today; I'd rather be there. But if I had not taken the unknown trail then I'd have no choice for today, because that is what opened my eyes to de-evolution of life in the America that I have known.

In my furies I have seen idiots rise to all that was promised for doing it as teachers taught as direction for living. I curse those who made such illegitimate promises. You all lied for saying, Follow *our wisdom and become all that we have.*

Hey, asswipes, all of what you have is broke, and even though I am a proven expert who owns wisdom for your needs… your measure of capacity to hire me is not available. These are my torments of frustration.

None of what I would instruct you towards is what all of you can or will accept. Even those who enjoy my generosity of limited nature will not hear. So the measure of my will has to change. I have sought the manipulations of my own greed to invite you. My blessings of being a man are not inviting enough. So what must I do other than to have faith? I have known wisdom was my asset, just as those in need have come to know my character, lives in matching any need. I have known this from my earliest days. My greatest fear now is that when you come to realize your own desperation of life or solution, I'll meet you by my corruptive tendency to exploit that need for my own twisted self interest. That will be the time when the purely innocent will be transgressed and I WILL lose favor in God's Witness. My appetite for hedonism and self gratification knows few limits, and that has also been written.

My partner of life suffers no fools. I am amazed she endures me. She convinces me that I am a good soul, so does her dog, and he is at my beckoning. She does so with one greater than my imagination, yet he holds an undeniable energy pulse. There can be no mistake of this man's wisdom to what calls me in stepping forward. His strength gives me faith greater than anything I ever claimed to know. I never talked shit about my capabilities and that is why I have my partner and gift from God in Tracy. Her friend introduced us to Pastor Paol and he need only ask. That is his credibility. He commands the angels in my life because even they are tired of my nitwittery… That is his job. It will be mine, but not yet.

Pastor Paol's circle is vast. The influence of those in faith with him could move a mountain. I spoke my rages and my words let loose a tempest upon his flock. And yet his wisdom remained steady. He, like I put faith in his pairing of partner. Denise his partner gave me her version of Hell for my speaking. I knew it was to come, but I also knew that what I said needed to be said. If nothing else, my rages allowed for discussion of everyone's troubles. My wisdom was never pretty or politically correct. Diplomacy is the promise of doing it to the result of being broke, and now it is time of leadership. Screw the stupid stuff. For all the experts who got us here... You can all kiss my ass. You can take all of your self protecting insurances of remaining in power and choke them. Men of faith and love of God are never accounted for in your measure of credit. Just as the Lord will come as a thief in the night so will works of faith go unseen without ledger's inscribing.

The judgment of man means nothing in the Kingdom of Heaven.

July 2, 2010

In the early days of summer, it has become exceedingly difficult for me to pay attention to any news that is being reported. Truly, the noteworthiness of what is being told has no noteworthiness at all. Moreover the depressing nature of the news is enough to break any healthy mentality one might possess.

As the days pass, I realize the genius of what I wrote in *Hypocronance* was greater than I could ever imagine. It seems that each day presents a revelation of more insanity, which becomes more acceptable. Just this morning, I read an article that was an accounting of how the BP oil spill cleanup crews do the job of cleaning beaches. There is a saying I find useful for the summation of what was presented in the article; "You can't make that kind of thing up."

A previous day I watched footage of a lone American in Phoenix who walked in a demonstration of the Arizona immigration law. He needed a police escort leading him away from hundreds, if not thousands of angry illegal aliens who would have likely torn the man to pieces in their rages.

Each day that passes leads me to believe that we will not avoid a violence coming. Those in control seem hell-bent on redefining our Country. The New World Order is busy and I mean very busy trying to dismantle traditions of centuries.

Yesterday I prayed on *wisdom*. I read scripture on wisdom and for the read I concluded that we as a people have turned away from truth in our dealings. Rage and anger have replaced logic and reason. Emotive tendency looses words and thoughts, which steal authority for justification as an afterthought. Today, people who made a previous decision hate the reality of the day for the decision made. Whether or not they can accept their own responsibility for making that decision is why I think the anger is so thick.

This was the immediate writing I put to paper after my praying on *wisdom*.

When we are faced with lack of leadership, we must stay steady and visit the past for what gave us greatness. Our founders, with reason gave us liberation to worship as we saw fit to suit our personal interest of that choice.

Our confusion of these days isn't insurmountable, nor can we continue in chaos. While I enjoyed a morning walk upon our Sound this morning and beheld the beauty of the environs, I wondered about the peril in the south eastern region. I asked my creator for wisdom so as to understand turmoil upon us.

Deuteronomy Chap 4 verse 5
Behold I have taught you statutes and judgments,
even as the Lord my God commanded me
that ye shall do so in the land whither ye go to
possess it.

Keep therefore and do them, for this is your wisdom
and your understanding in the sight of nations,
which shall hear all these statutes, and say, Surely
this great nation is a wise and understanding
people.

As I read these scriptures I heard the value of praising the Almighty God for delivering us ALL we have. The evidence, which is observable for this lack of leadership, cannot be mistaken. The absurdity of hearing all of those who claim to be just in the name of progressivism is plain, and they are not wise people. As the lord commanded us to follow his statutes, every value of progressivism suggests that they change the statutes for convenience.

And for doing these things of change, so many of us revaluate the greatness of our National Interest, knowing that until we return to them, our wisdom diminishes plainly for all nations to see. The current course of our Nation needs to change. We need to reinstate our Laws recognized as Under God.

It is difficult for me to imagine any people on this earth who would behold America as a nation of wise and understanding people today. Imagine if you might be an alien from another world, visiting us these days. What do you suppose that would be like?

Would you judge the human race as advanced in culture and wisdom, or barbaric, experiencing erosion of morality? It seems to me that the asylum is being run by the lunatics. Words like *racism* are being corrupted for the purposes of dismissing just laws of our land. I'm pretty sure that came to be vogue after President

Clinton argued the meaning what *sex* meant. He also made empty apology fashionable. I truly believe that standards of what used to be considered as appropriate, found the gravitational acceleration of a roller coaster's descent during the Clinton years.

Can a people who vote for hypocrites such as our recent leaders be thinking with reason or logic? Are we a great nation of wise and understanding people, or are we fools who would rather hear the claims of the frauds who'd tell us we are great and wise? Is our purpose one, which embraces electing criminals so we can enjoy seeking blame and then cast our vehemence without realizing the sin of being judgmental? Are we addicted to a conditioned response for ignoring our own responsibility as servants to each other?

I ask these questions because of our condition. We must know why we are here if we want to adjust our course to arrive at a different future. For me, I believe that as bad as it is now, it will get much worse. I believe this as our truth because I see beyond today. I have done this my whole life. I can envision the steps that deliver a wanted destination and I can heed a warning for steps leading to disaster. For the path we tread today as a people, I see nothing but disaster.

I came to understand that on a date in April something in the Gulf of Mexico was going to happen. This understanding is what all the folks who figure worst case scenarios might be. Right now they are drilling two relief valve wells for the releasing of pressure on the BP Horizon explosion that occurred on April 20th of this year.

There are many thoughts about this mess and what to do with it as well as what is yet to happen. I am pretty sure the worst case scenario will be the result. I pray I am wrong.

Worst case scenario results as a tsunami that will likely spread anywhere from 50-250 miles inland on coastal Gulf areas. To make matters worse the oil and dispersal agent named Corexit, will make all areas of land desolate. There is a media black out on how this disaster happened, but thanks to the internet there are a handful of courageous people who are doing the detective work to connect all the dots.

It is beginning to look like all the disaster and devastation is nothing more than exploiting profit for a handful of very greedy and evil people.

Now to make an assumption that relief drilling can be successful, when the first drilling was such a colossal failure is beyond any rational thinking I'd consider, but the hubris of these folks is beyond contemplation.

By the way, these are the same folks who are feeding the nitwittery for a Utopian world order, which wants to dismiss our Creator's place in our culture. They serve mammon and they claim to know God, and we all know how that goes.

July 2, 2010
12:11 PM

In these past weeks many have began to embrace a sense of difficulty coming. Some I know have met their soul mates while others have come to know the dread of inoperable disease. Others have discovered the lessening possibility of running ethical businesses, which have sustained their livelihood.

For all of these conditions of desperations and victories there is one common denominator. Those who care are drawing closer to their own spirituality. In the past two years my own prayer list has expanded to a number I could have never imagined. The intensity of faith shines, while the heat behind proselytizing and blaspheming cranks up. Diversions of chaos explode and the magic invisible hand brokers the deals that become law. The strength and audacity of tyranny grows while the finger pointing goes on and on. Those in power hope that man manipulating nature will torpedo the Constitutional process of voting all while they retain profits on the silent declaration of war against nature. The hubris of humanity tolerates the killing of the environment because the evil power in authority knows the selfish nature of those they rule.

In tyranny the enemy is always known in time's passage, and preventing corrective measure is better than the measure they apply for solving the issue; hence the Hypocronance of Media.

About a month ago two men were assassinated by our law enforcement and they were American labeled as *terrorists*. It was a father and son team and the news reported on it as it just happened. Breaking News!

Tyranny of men suppresses free speech, while supporting militant doctrine claiming that it does so for vanquishing evil perceived from the corrupt whores of media and their propaganda. How else could the resurgence of the Black Panthers occur? The truth of all of this hell is left to one solution. We as rugged individualists need to make the changes required in attaining the solution of our own condition. We can not get lost in our petty semantics of policy. We must discern the issues correctly without the peddlers of mediocrity; we must determine objectives.

Tea Party folks are forming a type of doctrine, but it is home grown. It lacks solidarity of a nation, thusly those in power command their 'paids' to harass and belittle the initiative. Why else would there be so many articles on the growing abundance of unsettled folks finding inclusion on the ten guidelines of the movement?

The Tea Party Movement was promised as being radical, yet where is the radical proof to suggest such an ideology?

There is none. No the evidence supports otherwise. It supports a movement the tyranny underestimated. Moreover it supports a willingness to deny and even sabotage the movement with underhanded violence. Violence is implemented at gatherings affording the right to convene for grievance in our Constitution. Those guilty of the inciting are never prosecuted and likely paid very well for their loyalty to the enemy.

I find myself bitter for the two-party system. For the life of me, I don't understand why men can't come up with thinking that embraces more points of view in debating policies. Granted, my tendency is conservative, but I wouldn't count myself as GOP. Pure Liberal thinking is worth listening to, but socialist thinking isn't acceptable in the realm of capitalism. Socialism doesn't have need for individuality and if individuality of rugged nature isn't allowed for, than it should find another place to dwell. This is America, folks, and the world has looked to our innovative nature throughout our history.

These days I imagine the world watches in terror as we bungle this oil spill. The Deep Water

Horizon disaster has the potential to be a world ender. Socialism of Obama's liking isn't allowing the best thinkers to come to this problem. There is one reason for that too, and that reason is greed. Sometimes I wonder what could be going on in the man's head. Does he think that folks believe his bullshit? Is he in full faculty, or is he out of his mind? It is difficult to imagine him as the leader he thinks he is, for that matter, I do believe he is a puppet who listens to directives based upon formative decisions he made, while perceiving injustices being raised as a communist. His parents were indeed communists. How far does the apple fall from the tree?

The sum of the problem isn't just Obama. There is a considerable burden of our condition granted to us by the legislative branch as well. Our Congress is certainly up to this to their necks in accountability. The largest contributors give them thirty pieces of silver many, many times as they become career politicians. For those contributions they began usurping the oaths of office they take to become politicians, and think nothing of it. Yesterday Nancy Pelosi said, "Unemployment checks are the greatest means to promote job growth." I kid you not.

That is her wisdom on how to bail a sinking ship out; instead of allowing prosperity of the tax payer she wants to see that the tax payer becomes the recipient of tax revenues that will never be met. The woman is an idiot, and she leads the

House. Harry Reid is another imbecile. He was in trouble over declaring income. Both of these individuals couldn't come up with one sound idea concerning the general welfare of our country if they had a map and a flashlight. Yet they remain in office and we must ask why and how?

Might it be that those who are influential with money are pulling their strings? Might it be a case of owing folks so as to get favor for legislation? We are promised transparency of disclosure, but when bureaucracy is the oversight of ethics manipulated by those in power, what transparency can there be? For instance, Obama's cabinet appointees couldn't be vetted for their jobs as they had pending tax issues, yet they would be overseeing tax increases on all they governed. How does that happen? Who designs such flagrant betrayal of the purpose to be in office?

It is my contention that the voters need to be savvier about casting their ballot. They should look to someone who can't be bought off. How do you go about such a thing? I'm not sure. Having suffrage for our allotment of population is an incredible dilemma.

One party wants to say they'll help those who won't or can't help themselves, while the other says that those who hold the wealth should be rewarded for offering employment under less government oversight. How do you convince someone without life skills that it is up to them to provide for themselves? How do you correct wrongly perceived notions of whether life is supposed to be fair or not? All of these things have been given ripeness from an industry that knows how to mesmerize folks with an irresistible addiction by making them feel better or worse for their own conditions.

Hypocronance is what I called the dynamic that got folks to believe in the BS and pit them against each other for the purpose of controlling the masses. Socialists may want the country to fall with a determination of one world government. The more I think on it, the more it becomes evident that they need America to fail. Then they can abscond with the wealth and resource of the nation and become monarchs of the world. Europe is now in the throws of falling. Hell, those countries can't come up with a ratifiable Constitution to claim unity. That much is fact. So the belief that America is bad has been bought and sold to those wanting to stay on top and those who wish for just a bit more than their slice of pie.

When those who came to America did so, they left the persecutions of the old world to forge a new world. Why would we ever think it would be good to go back to the old ways, unless of course the fiction we were creating didn't reveal the end of monarchy?

So it must be time to go back to basics. Men are capable of many things. Just because we are capable doesn't mean that we can ignore natural truths. The natural truth of our culture is the fact that we designed our world to be free under a guideline of laws. That didn't come from democracy. It came from a republic. Democracy is the dictation of the mob and if we want to know what that is all we have to do is go to Phoenix and watch the criminals demand naturalization for inclusion based on the predication that The United States of America pays you to exist here. Not only do you get to exist here, but there is extra reward for repopulating more of your ignorant kind.

After the media had demonized Bush, they pat themselves on the back for giving an unqualified black man the most important job in the world. That isn't a racial slur by the way, it is purely fact. That swell of support came because the media had forgotten its purpose or even worse than forgetting, they deceived their own ends of purpose for thinking Utopia was a potential reality. Most democrats in the days of racial equity wanted to deny full citizenship for those of color. That is also fact. So now the same socialist ilk from then decided that installing a dope, who could be made the fool was the map to the treasure they couldn't find themselves. A year and a half after the fact it is coming apart and it is getting worse by the second.

The Founding Fathers were no newbie's to a poker table and these men came to the debate floor in Philadelphia and hammered out arguments to devise a better form of governance so that the individual could flourish. The debate was fierce in the heat of the summer days and they came up with our Bill of Rights and ultimately the beginning of a Constitution, which bound the federal government to insure the individual rights of citizens over states rights to govern. What we have arrived at would make the Founding Fathers slap everyone in representation today.

Where do we go from here? How do we reclaim our right to freedom as a people? Should we write legislation of more bad laws, or should we consider repealing unneeded laws or laws that minimize our freedoms as individuals? As a voter, what are you thinking? As a citizen, what do you see your responsibility to be for the process of elections? Are we as citizens supposed to think for our own condition as individuals or consider the welfare of our culture as individuals who govern themselves? These are considerations that are no longer taught in the system of education. If you examine the policy of today, you'll see that being American costs nothing, it is free for no effort. Better than that, why not just forget America and sing Kum-bah-yah in worldwide harmony? The media is certainly keeping an eye on the possibility of more peddling of their addiction product. In America we have 300+ million viewers. They might as well consider the possibility of an audience numbering 6 billion. Better ratings, ya know.

The question facing us for this guarantee of our collective sovereignty is who do we put into office for the election coming in November? Now before you say what you feel, are you going to consider the importance of this question? Better yet, how should we come to consider this question? Now, I know there is no book of directions on how to be a good parent, and I never saw a book on what it was explaining the responsibility of being a concerned citizen. But as a free people these are critical thinking questions, which need answering. How do you go about selecting the right person for the job? Where do you find belief in those promising to do what they promise for your vote? The reality is blatantly painful that in this last election none of the promises given were kept. In fact, the whole thing was a terrible fiction of a future that could never be paid for as a Utopia.

So once again, how do we arrive at a better decision? Do we listen to those entrusted with the Constitutional power of information dispersal? The Main Stream Media has given birth to what I have named Hypocronance. So, you see, it isn't just a party vote. It isn't a snap decision. We can't afford any more popularity votes. I sure do know that our country cannot withstand another puppet

President, nor can it withstand the socialist representation of a majority of our Congress.

As voters and people responsible for our own governance as a republic, I know of three ways to make changes needed to be made. The first and, of course most preferable is to vote wisely. That gives us the second way to manage change, which comes through legislative process for impeachment of the Commander in Chief. The third is troubling but definitely on the table and that is a Military Coup. These are the tools under the words within the Constitution that we can use as lawful citizens to undo a bad choice of leadership. There is also a possibility of an unlawful change in power and as we know by history. 4 times President's were killed. That is not one of my suggestions, it couldn't be as I love my country too much, never the less it is a reality.

Do we vote one party out for the sake of replacing them with maybe another party that is guilty of selling us down the road in times coming? Keep in mind that both parties have produced both good and bad public servants. What we need to face our future isn't just good public service, what we need are excellent leadership skills.

Given that we as a people have become apathetic to the condition we now know, is it even possible to think that we are capable of selecting a proper representation? So, what do we collectively think? Do we figure it out as we digest the suggestions from the whores of media? Or, do we reach deep in our figuring to become ready for the vote?

July 5, 2010
7:48:10 AM

Independence Day is behind us and the time ahead grows even shorter. In an email I received there was a YouTube link that offered an Anderson Cooper report. He works for CNN, which is one of the organizations within the MSM. Mr. Cooper's main theme of the report was about accessibility the media had to cover The Gulf Oil Spill. He was largely complaining about prohibition from BP and USCG oversight. He was also reiterating the justification of purpose the media was beholden to in the Constitutional framework.

In the book *Hypocronance* I discussed how the MSM would cherry-pick news and report it so as to forward their own agenda as they did in favoring Senator Obama when he was running for office. I also spoke to the time when those same cherry-pickers of the news would continue to support the man until his ineptitude and incompetence could no longer abide it. And in the report by Anderson Cooper, my prediction was substantiated.

To be fair to Mr. Cooper he wasn't named in *Hypocronance*. Generally speaking I think he is one of the guys who 'gets it'. Here is the thing; the spill happened April 20th. It is July 5th and these reports are the first exposures to the incompetence of crisis management. As the summer moves on we'll hear more of the media complaints regarding the insanity that they themselves saw to delivering. After all, the public wants accounting for the trouble in the Gulf.

Consider Katrina... within a week the press was demanding that President Bush wasn't doing enough. If you are honest and reasonable, you can only conclude that the media is biased. If you don't see that, then you truly are in the folly of hypocronance.

Even today as we face this environmental nightmare is the media doing enough to inform the public of just what Congress and the administration are doing?

Why isn't the media demanding from Congress transparency for not passing a budget? That is the duty of Congress as it is written in law. So why isn't the media demanding this? Might it be that their favored agenda would be exposed as unimaginably ridiculous for the cost associated to the course of policy?

Why don't the media hammer the issue of unemployment, or even a greater tax burden coming for next year? It is because they can't. It would expose them as a greater part of the problem that we all face. They wanted this socialism. But the tyranny of their Utopia now prevents them from the decision of embracing socialism and they win for it by condemning policy as it prevents them from the original intent of their job.

That brings us back to where we arrived at before.... How do we as a people choose a commonality for the purposes of installing better representation?

Do we allow a continuance on a wealth redistribution type of thinking, which has produced nothing but failure for the last three and a half years? Is it not clear that government stimulus is a disaster for the cost? At what point do we make a commitment to say, "We made a mistake and it is time to have a correction implemented."

Obama is suing five states now. He is in legal trouble up to his eyeballs in court proceedings to prove his citizenship status so as to be a valid president and he has apparently profited for association with those wrapped up in the dealings of companies that are criminal.

The same companies who benefited for the stimulus are still benefiting from the environmental crisis as it still happens. Reports are available that follow the money all the way back to campaign donations made to Obama. You won't hear about it from the MSM either. You do have to do a bit of research, but it is out there.

In this coming election there will be many races run to office. There is no way to speak to all of the candidates as who will be better to send because of the needs concerning state's rights. It is incumbent on folks to rise and support whoever is unable to be bought off by those seeking to influence special interests.

How do we achieve such a decision? There is no easy way to do this. You have to study who seeks a vote for your representation and become involved. You have to make a judgment about those who would serve your ideal of better leadership. So WE as voters need to engage the process. It is the most important thing we will do as a nation. If we don't get this decision right, I fear the greatness and blessing of what we are will be permanently surrendered to an irreparable condition. The only possibility after that for reclaiming our heritage would likely come at the end of another civil war.

It is my estimation that the Tea Party Movement is the best thinking of the day concerning a common sense type of approach to managing our nation. The truth of the Tea Party movement is exactly what both camps of DC and the media have consistently named as anything but sensible.

The Tea Party movement represents local initiatives going to a federal capacity. Folks, that is how our governance is supposed to work; we send our reps to do OUR business. Lately, Federal Authority comes before the people. The New World Order speaks without American interests, while it steals our wealth to fund projects for international business and governance. It got this way because Americans forgot their place; we are the board of directors making demands for our government. It happened because of hypocronance. The marriage of representation and constituency was corrupted by the whores of media. That bit of wisdom is what we all need to think about for making the decision we face.

What do you think Oprah Winfrey knows about running a country? Wasn't she one in the political process of getting Obama elected? Isn't she a power player in the world of MSM? Where is her voice now that Obama is a miserable failure, incapable or unwilling to live up to his promises? The last I heard anything about Oprah in the news was when she was condemning folks who thought Jesus Christ was our savior. She kept saying that there was more than one way to be redeemed. She can't speak to Obama as she did support him, so her next gig is to do what? Argue a principle of theocracy, which wants to move away from what gave us our blessings as a country.

Where is the anguish in Oprah's heart for our south eastern neighbors facing this crisis? Is she using her platform to condemn BP and demand more transparency for a government responsible to manage the greatest man made disaster likely ever known? No, of course she isn't. Yet so many folks listened to her judgment about a man who hasn't been what she sold him to be.

The *emotive vote* is our biggest enemy. It doesn't consider reason; it considers matters of the heart. When you make a vote based upon a willingness of mob thinking, what do you expect for the result? When you make a vote on who will best suit your particular thinking on important issues, then we will have better governance. That is why the system was designed the way it is. Those who want term limits don't grasp that the vote should be the term limit. Legislating for stupidity isn't a good idea. Legislating to create more bureaucracy is even a worse idea, yet we seem to do it all the time.

How is it possible to vote upon a 2,000 page bill in a matter of days? How is it possible to even create such a document? I am a prolific writer and I can't imagine writing such a thing. I can hardly get anyone to read a well crafted fiction that is 200 pages in length. Yet millions of tax payer dollars are spoken to in these unread monstrosities known as bills.

Let me ask you something; Suppose you are managing your household, or a business and your town sends you in the mail a notification that because it so sees fit as an authority, you'll have to spend half of your budget towards investment that does you no profitability. In the case of owning a home you'd need to come up with the funds to update your house immediately or you won't be able to sell it. See, that is a law they want to pass. Or in the case of a business you now have to become entangled in a government run health insurance, forcing you to pay for something you may have not needed. That is what the feds are up to and there is more... In 2011 the Bush tax cuts will expire and everyone, including the lowest paid wage earners will be liable to income taxation greater in liability than we know now. Their policy does nothing for improving the likelihood to create jobs. The unintended consequences for an emotive vote are lagging awareness. They always cost more and they demand more of a contribution. So if you voted for something, which sounded too good to be true... the reality is what we have today.

Getting back to what should be rules of thumb in considering who to vote for in the coming elections I would advise that you ask one question. Is one on the ticket is an incumbent? Check the record and see if they voted for the stimulus package... if they did, they need to be fired! Now, on the other hand ask a new candidate if they would go to office looking to repeal the laws written of this last congress and signed by the current President. None of those laws written are sustainable, nor are they likely valid.

Because I am of an individual mind I'd ask you to have a peek at this YouTube link; http://www.youtube.com/watch?v=XwG5MhVGQ6k

This is what I speak to in *Hypocronance*. These are influential people who have turned their backs on the oath every service member takes. That oath includes defending the Constitution of America as well as their state constitution of residence. The whores of media don't want to align themselves for abiding the Constitution, because the Constitution won't tolerate injustice of a powerful minority.

Listen carefully to the star power's ability to exploit semantics. Everything they said sounded good, but it came for a price, which is too good to be true. Honestly, which one of any of those pledges is worth anything? Maybe this can be a valued lesson for those who were hoodwinked for their emotive tendency? Maybe you'll grow up and realize running the country can't be done because of a popularity vote. Running a country for the general welfare of the people isn't as easy as folks think. The promise to make a better world is the responsibility of all of us. It can't be the promise of one man seeking a vote. We don't hear any of the same supporting Obama, now that the proof has been revealed.

You will hear about their new fangled ideas as distractions concerning this President or for the oath they took. But will one of them dare to say they were wrong? Once again, witness the folly of hypocronance. When it comes time for you to cast your vote, you can't allow those who are clueless about the job of running our country to be your guiding investment as research needed to inform yourself. You do realize that those in the above video are who they are because of one thing... their value as entertainers, right? You do realize that these folks need scripts and that they bring to you humor or fictional accounts designed to make your life easier. Are they aware of what a Commander in Chief considers concerning life and death every day? Of course they aren't, if they didn't have a script, or a director, or even a good graphic art team, you'd never pay the money for the ticket price spent in making your own reality just a little bit more forgettable. Yet they are the mouthpiece for the nitwits who glorify them selves as cool folks who *have* to know better.

7/5/2010 1:27 PM

I want to shift course here a bit. I want you to think of what you would tell your friend or even just a business associate if they asked for your thoughts on somebody you might refer for a service they needed. Would you be a person who would claim to know a credible concern that they might need and offer that referral based upon not knowing, or would you give them the benefit of your experience?

Think on that question, because if another seeks your wisdom and it results badly for them; you own their indignation. I have come to the wisdom I speak of concerning referrals because my own advice or others' I sought have cost more than the value of the advice. Those can be friend-breaking deals. And if the value of offering the advice is great, it can be one of those things that comes back at you threefold to your hurt.

The burden of giving folks advice they don't want to hear is weight many don't want to carry. The only upstroke to giving them advice they don't want to hear is when those seeking the advice are paying you as a consultant. See, when you give folks advice they don't want to hear and time passes, proving the advice you gave as accurate, well, that gives everybody gets a good dose of senior memory slips. Only when they pay for the advice does it seem like a good idea; a Value for investment of heeding the wisdom. Then the advice becomes better as a referral and more valuable for taking a risk that paid off.

Many can see me as a crazy bastard, because I don't care what you think of me, I really don't. You either accept me as I am, or ya can get on line to kiss my ass. There is one truth I abide. I will offer you any help I can to improve your condition or strengthen your reasoning if you seek it and here is why; because once you know the value of the advice I offer, you will seek it out and then we can negotiate the value of the advice you need.

That is how I do things in my life. Hell, I've given days of labor away for the price of feeding me and supplying me with smokes and beer. Never once in those arrangements has anyone ever felt slighted on my behalf.

Here is the thing, unless you can teach me something I don't know, or unless I'm seeking your wisdom... I don't care what you think. The reason I write this piece is because that being stupid or emotive for the upcoming election isn't gonna do any of us any good. If you want to live in the best place on the globe, you better make sure that your decision-making is less of what you feel and more of what you know. I am tired of window-lickers telling me what I don't know, even after I have presented evidence to possessing more wisdom than they will ever be able to argue.

So here it is - If you can tell me of a better way, I'll listen. But if that better way is based upon what you think, rather that what I already know to be true... you are gonna be schooled. And if you resent it, then have at it. Unless you can prove me wrong, I won't give up my convictions in knowing how to arrive at a better general welfare for the people in the country I love, called these United States of America. And to those Hollywood nitwits who took the oath to Obama, none of ya will ever work on any of my material, and that is final. And for seeing the oath from the takers, there is one who might be able to carry the role off. You too, can kiss my ass.

Here is why I don't care... Get over to Amazon.com and type my name in on a search. Keep in mind when you see the vast amount of material under my name it came to be within a year to a year and a half. Read it and leave a commentary. I have done more writing across more genres than any librarian can speak to and that is a fact. I actually owe Obama and the progressive nitwit socialists a great big thank you. If it weren't for them I would have literally had paying work that would have made that writing impossible. So it is with unemployment. Those who can do, get it done, and those who can't or won't, teach or suck of the milk of democracy. I took six months of earned unemployment and was denied the federal extension, and by as long as my days are numbered here on this earth I won't take one dime from this abortion of a bureaucracy our country has come to be. I have offered the option to sell books at huge reductions to our veterans abroad and networked with the turncoat politicians. They gave me the number to call, which was never responded to even after several inquiries. And yes, Joe Lieberman... you have given me great disappointment in your stewardship of our Constitution. I thought you to be a better man, but you aren't the bag of potato chips you claimed to be. You are full of hot air. I gave many chances at offering wisdom to harness... by the by, nobody paid attention. And as we do get onto the writing of why this vote is critical to remain Americans, let us examine exactly what is in the middle of it all.

Political Correctness.

Short of emotive voting... wait... emotive voting is the product of political correctness. Sometimes I get ahead of myself.

Political correctness gave us affirmative action. And if anyone thinks that is a good idea... burn this book! I mean it. You will learn nothing for reading these words.

In my days of working, there were some jobs I had to get on for a paycheck, which required union membership. Now if most folks knew of hiring a labor lawyer or even of the LRB, unions wouldn't even have a need. But because I was married to a liberal emotive voter, she convinced me to take the work. I never saw such a cluster fuck attacking productivity in my life. So-called men would sabotage their own P.P.E. to make a point that management couldn't maintain insurance protocol. And these silly bastards who called themselves men, bitched to the heavens like a sewing bee of old lady quilters. They also collected the same rate of pay I did without any skills I possessed. But the tune goes on, until we had this Messiah elected office because everyone wants a hand grab in the circle jerk of black slavery that apparently still lives! Excuse me! I worked with all colors of folks and not once did I ever make attribution of job performance to skin color. In MY job everyone bled the same color. In my job everyone bled; and that was dealt with by using Dunkin' Donut Napkins along with electrical tape or duck tape as required.

The only damn things that got ya in trouble on my jobs were slacking or stupidity. It was never, ever skin color. When you suggested productivity slow downs or sabotage of company material... you might be needing the same first aid we provided and without having an accident. Those were the rules and on my jobs I was king of king's.

But this affirmative action; never happened under my authority. Nor will it ever.

So what do we have right now here in this country while we consider the vote coming?

Okay let's try this: What is America intolerant towards? Name one place on this globe where you can come and learn what it is to be American and believe any faith you want? Short answer.... No where.

Another example?

Let's ask this, where else can you violate the law and have a reality to present a defense that offers mitigating circumstances, which could find you innocent? Yet we have those here who suggest we are an evil people. Shit, we even give options to criminals. Did you know on the southern border of Mexico, they use a deterrent that our court would admonish? I mean, is it just me, or do you realize that America is the only place in the world that has a measure of equality matched nowhere else in the world?

Need more?

Why are the most profitable countries in the world learning English? Shortest answer: The American public is the easiest group of fat folks to profit on for learning another language.

All you need to do is enslave your own people and sell Americans cheap products. Why? Because they have walked away from their principles of quality and ethical business for aggressive takeovers and short profits, all while our sense of morality disappears.

Christians spoke of loving thy neighbor.

Who are your neighbors? Do you even know them? While we design Scientology to imbue ourselves with arrogant pride, what have we forgotten? Why do we need to create *escape fiction* so as not to honor laws of thousands of years that gave rise to great nations?

Trivia check?

What in these US States is the largest money making Business? Hmmm…. Green industry? No. Government Expenditure? No. Technology or even medicine? No. The largest industry with the highest profits is PORN. It even outdoes drug profits.

Hell, any good cash businessman would exploit both drugs and sex and be better off than Bernie Medoff. Yeah, the same bitch who robbed so many Hollywood types. The more the folks open their mouths; the more you come to realize how the good Lord gave wealth out in portions. They may look good, but without a script they'd be grazing in a field.

So our country and western world walks away from truth in faith. We possess pride and forget why we have our blessings and in the orgy of circle jerks and profits of nitwittery. Then we sit alone paying the therapists for unknown ailings.

Screw the apothecaries of old, we want the new stuff. We want that which will make us cool. Shit, even soothsayers of youthful promise sell it, all while we ignore that which gave us our very virtue. Virtue spoke of something not available to purchase without rightness of two simple things.

It offered us glory in life and perfection thereafter, but our amortization just didn't make it a worthwhile following, or investment.

You see, we will be the first generation of a people who has less than our parents. The sin isn't ours alone, but it is ours. If we give in to this NWO we devolve. The fairness of socialism or communism is a lie. Our greatness was purchased by those who knew the things they did would pay for the salvation for those that followed.

Kinda like Christ.

He said, honor thy God as they Father, and love thy neighbor as you would love yourself. In cities today, shootings dictate nobody knew any of each other. Our idols are those who need scripts for delivery of meaning; keeping us interested in lies that promise us nothing except fifteen seconds of what we want worship, but will never invest towards.

We give harbor and safety to those we'd condemn for the violence they preach, we usurp our heritage as indulged righteous folks became bored with works that mean something. We claim we love our brothers and sisters while we scream to the heavens and condemn the works of the faithful, calling them followers of a myth and we wonder why it is that we have the difficulties we have.

If we judge, shall we not be judged ourselves?

If we lead, shall we not be followed? And if we do lead it is only because we possess that gift for purpose. If our following is led to desperation, what is the sum of such desperation worth?

What possession shall we judge to be worthy when we convince others that their need is greater than our own to lead them to us? Would it be fame? Would it be transference of worth greater than what we could possess ourselves? Are we so inclined to remove our own position to benefit another?

You see my friends, my countrymen; what we have at our hands is divine reality just as our forefathers knew to come. This is the reason that OUR system was designed in the manner that followed. We are a great and good people, it is written in all of our history. As a good people we have done things to enrich ourselves at the cost of others. That much is true. While we face this crisis in the Gulf, we need to remember that we owe nothing to anybody. Our place in life has repeatedly risen to the call of sacrifice for nothing but loss, except for the ability to shine in the love of man as we understood; paying for it as a country under GOD. Our Constitution allowed us to know our faith, and that is ample for the world!

We love our forgotten pasts, we have made mistakes but we also know that to deliver anything less than we possess, would be a sin. That would expose all of our undoing as it will on the Day of Judgment, but what we need to remember as AMERICANS is that we knew freedom here as Americans. And for being free, everyone else wanted the same. All we asked is that you convict yourself to our fairness in life. If you can't, then you must die for your own because right now we must retake what is being sold away. Hollering in the streets and abducting forgotten principle based on singular motivation is passed. Many of us realize now that without the love of who we are, we as a country are unsustainable and that is a bad place to be. We can handle lies, we can even cheat ourselves, but when the time comes; when we have to figure on our past...we'll realize that a sleeping Giant has awoke, and the trickery of your dream-weaving will be analyzed and digested.

Sons and daughters, rise to your heritage and claim the virtue that beckons your anger of today. The enemy is coming and you won't be who you are if you submit... Take this from the fatherless father who meant you nothing but the love he couldn't give while sending it along with the Christmas promise of gifts yet to come.

Be civil minded as you can, but forget not that blood might need to flow. We are better than anyone else, and that has also been proven, but if it comes to sacrifice, I hope you summon Memorial Day and bring the hope of *the fallen* with you. They wanted nothing less than to dare you to have a vote. MAKE your vote upon your wisdom of error!

Praise the bounty of our land... these United States of America, where even our freedom gave our enemies a place to call home.

And keep with Jesus as he said, "I have paid your sins for ascension to my place in heaven." Two rules, keep it simple.

7/8/2010
1:36 PM

More earthquakes are happening. California has had a couple if not three. Another occurred in the south east to Canada and another in Okalahoma. It is day 80 and the oil still flows.

It flows at an estimated 2.5 million gallons a day. Imagine the void below and try to reckon what that means for tectonic plates. What replaces the oil as it escapes? If there is no replacement will the ground not find the law of gravity? While the oil flows, low and medium food chains die.   There are those who still think BP and Obama's administration aren't profiting on this disaster. Even when Bill Ayers made reference to exploiting a disaster those who are reluctant to acknowledge facts remain in denial.

In the past days we have seen oil deposits left on cars during precipitation. Folks said that *raining oil* was impossible. Just the other day YouTube videos showed people swimming in the waters of the Gulf. They claimed not to have seen any oil around until they were shown the oil where they claimed none was. It is beyond my understanding why so many will not see this crisis for what it is. Maybe they just can't process it and the easy thing to do is choose ignorance.

Earlier today during some errands, Tracy and I discussed a conversation she had with a driver at work. She told me that Brandon informed her that he read my notes at Facebook; he also thought that I didn't like Obama too much at all. After more discourse he told her that he in fact did vote for Obama because he was a 'Brother'. Brandon himself is black. Tracy asked Brandon, "How's that Obama vote workin' out for ya now?" Brandon informed her that he hates the choice he made, because the guy is killing us.

Couple of things here; First of all, I had nothing but hope that Obama would do the things he promised, and I gave him every opportunity to prove my skeptical leaning wrong. Secondly, I can see a dynamic, which leaves abundant evidence that our education system sucks. You see, even when people are shown evidence of unpleasant and troubling observation, they will remain in denial, and more importantly they will vote for less than self informed reason.

In our history people struggled to attain suffrages, even if it meant their deaths. Today the vote is nothing more than a notion of popularity and worse, the feds are giving votes away to insure they have an abundance of emotive minded voters. The value of our free citizenry is being diminished and it erodes for laziness, greed and stupidity. *Hypocronance* defined the dynamic and explained how we arrived here. And those who helped make the past are now being sought out for solutions of our problems. How do we not get back into the other issues of the past if we seek the wisdom of immediate past?

Conservatives listen to Dick Morris and Newt Gingrich. Dick Morris was the advisor to the Clintons and Newt was Speaker of the House during the Clinton administration. How does anyone think either of these two guys has a plan that won't end up in a closer swing of the pendulum in another five years? They argue what any student of the plainly observable can see, but are they speaking to cures that you haven't heard before?

One thing I have come to know about myself in all my years is this: Whenever I face injury, at the end of my thinking on it; I am the one responsible for my own injury. Sure, somebody may have acted negligently and maybe even grossly so, but if I hadn't been there when they were acting so grossly in negligence, I would have never been injured. So, I reason similarly to the occasion of having Obama and these socialist pigs running our government, I allowed it to happen because I didn't do enough to prevent it.

In my experience of the last twenty years, I thought that telling people the results for their thinking of the day would be appreciated. Most of the time it largely went unheard, and my anger grew for frustration by being the guy who says, "I told ya so." So, maybe I should have spoken less and made a difference by running for office. But there again, for my own actions of habit, I wasn't even close to being electable. Even if I had a successful bid and won the office, I would have been railroaded or killed because I don't give a shit about so called power players. The likelihood is I would have been framed or killed by the machinations of those in power.

In our system, we have two significant parties with splinter groups that won't amount to victory in a majority. Now in between the 2 parties we have about 55% that are called independent voters. 55% of voters figure by identity that they fall somewhere in liking what the Tea Party Movement has to say. Any of your larger polling groups suggest that as fact of polling. If nothing else the result of Obama will make this next congress more aligned for Tea Party thinkers to install like-minded candidates into representation.

Do you believe in Constitutional Process? Do you believe that the indignation of a people can hold a leader or leadership accountable? Will the ineffective leadership implement laws before the installation of newly elected officials, which would leave us beyond repair?

So, what else then is left? How do we see these midterm elections while a greater portion of folks will likely vote not seeing reality as it presents itself? Moreover, how do we manage those who want to elect namesakes of the past for the convenience of not offering courage for some new thinking?

What do we do?

We are all unhappy, yet we seek the good times of the past as we tune into these idiots everyday. So what do we do? Who has the great ideas? Who knows American bureaucracy and who knows what Americana beholds?

How is it that lawyers can subvert the legislative duties by judicial civil activism? How is it that we can dismiss debate of a majority for the greed of a minority? How is it that we can rewrite laws so that the criminal has more rights than a victim? And finally how is it that we can continue to call ourselves a great nation when such chaos abounds?

Somebody elected Obama. And someone before him who was loved made apologies consequence free. Bill Clinton wagged his finger very parochially and mandated his forgiveness because it was owed to him. He made apology without penance acceptable.

So, if you voted for Obama and find yourself asking *WTF was I thinking?*, you need to speak up and own the mistake. You need to write letters of disapproval. Call your media and say enough of this! Consequence free apologies ain't getting it done. Unless those of you who fainted, or felt cleansed for voting for Obama retract your choice publicly, I fear the country is in mighty peril.

Those of us who figured him as presented knew it was gonna be bad, but we never thought his audacity would include wiping out an entire region of the country.

Billy Ayers, that scumbag, self serving bitch had conversations that spoke to the genocide of 30 million people almost forty years ago. He spoke to those of us who would retaliate in the face of a new world order. Now in the desert they are building body vaults for internment conditions of the genocide they spoke to, and for what they are doing, the half-wits underestimated the need.

Try to imagine the results of a hurricane like Katrina hitting the Gulf Coast with all these toxins in the water as they are. Fuel will be miles inland.

Corexit will also be in the same area. Now maybe you don't know what that means... maybe you do. Wherever that toxic water finds itself, land will be desolated. Think of radiation. Think of no plant growth. Think of insect and animal deaths. You see, it may not even matter if the elections ever happen. If nature has her way... we may never have another election again.

So let me ask ya again, "How is the progressive vote workin' out for ya?" Was this your idea of Utopia? One quarter of our country may be gone for this Utopia. Is that what you wanted, because the guy was a brother?

When you folks wake up you'll realize racism in the States doesn't exist as it does elsewhere in the world. You hate mongers just need to go to the southern border of Mexico to know what that is... there they shoot those illegally crossing the border.

Semantics of words aren't good enough. Deceit of thinking can no longer be manipulated. The time of feel-good living has just got notified and the bank of morality is foreclosing. The same ass-clown you elected is negotiating borrowing with competitors, all while he taxes you with interest on the debt.

People like George Soros, who are driven to their monetary substance know no morality. These are the people making decisions for you who sold Obama. If Soros had to compensate your ass to support Obama it may as well have been thirty pieces of silver. And all the while the same honest folks are kept down possessing better creativity than you would ever know.

Example? Here you go. Why is *Eclipse*, the saga of Twilight making more money than any other movie in the summer time market? Seriously, why do you think it is making the box office records?

Might it be because it is pure mystique or oblivious fiction? Might it be that you'd love to have the powers of either a werewolf or vampire? Might it be that you just don't want to know your own reality? A reality fantasized without having to think about living better? I haven't seen the movies, nor will I likely do so until it goes to cable. I wonder if like traditional vampire flicks, it speaks to divine weaponry as the only power to defeat the evil beasts.

Probably not, it used to be that vampires could only be thwarted by divinity. Who knows, today? As far as the Hollywood nitwits care, God should be dead. They work overtime to minimize our national trust under God. It is an affront to their being. So while we listen to all these feel good folks in the biggest orgy of humanity since Sodom and Gomorrah, is it any surprise that we are killing ourselves?

Over the past couple of days Lindsay Lohan went before a judge and got 180 days for violating her probation. If you have followed it in the MSM, they are sweating her case out like it was the priority of the day. A starlet of the MSM's mourning; they embrace judgment of her own indignation for our laws. We are losing an entire eco-system and all they can do is talk about some chick, who had the pearl of the world in her hands, but decided to keep her head in a coke bag and think a Judge was an unserious person to face.

Hey, Lindsay! Nitwit! When a Judge tells ya how it is... Don't think ya know better! Is the MSM telling you of food price inevitabilities for the Gulf oil spill? NO! How about the reality of evacuating some 40 million people? No.

Those whores want to give the public one vision of poor Lindsay tearfully disbelieving the disproof of her Utopia. And you'd rather watch that, than consider certain trouble ahead. Now maybe we can consider that our education system is screwed.

Critical Thinking is the enemy to progressive thought.

Critical thinking skills catch nitwit progressives like deer in headlights of an on coming car in a moonless night. What amazes me is they all think they are better than the moth consumed by the flame. And they just keep doing it.

Obama spoke on the Martin Luther King anniversary. His supporters called those of us who disagreed with him racists. Who are the biggest players in the details of his cabinet? The Black Panthers. How does anyone justify such a position? It seems that everything the left says serves convenience of the moment. When you are justifying time by the clock, there is no production for the negotiated contract of delivery for compensation.

Obama and his cronies are the undisputed enemies of individuals wanting to be entrepreneurs. He wants all of their profit and control for just showing up and the idiots who gave him his mandate forgot the value of being employee. This stuff was written in the scriptures, folks. The same scriptures our forefathers knew writing the Constitution.

The kids he hoodwinked into America's Jobs Core who are cleaning up his oil spill are gonna be worse off than Viet Nam vets who handled and were exposed to Agent Orange. Nobody is working in the area with the proper PPE. How's that for genocide? Don't worry; the survivors will be covered under his national health care bill just like the vets are under another government subsidized bureaucracy. You remember how the left condemned Bush when the vets' hospital was falling down under his watch... Right? You know, Walter Reed Veterans' Hospital? So what poor hospital is gonna take care of all of these bribed kids doing the clean up?

I wonder... I wonder if folks have a fear. Do they fear being offensive and then do they fear being righteous? If you thought to be offensive, it may have been a good idea to vote for Obama. But if you won't speak to the error of the vote, are you fearful of being righteous? In life we all make mistakes. That is as sure as the nose on your face. But if we don't acknowledge the mistakes of our judgment, where do we dwell? Are we cowards in the shade of evidenced light? Do we carry the weight of denying thrice our service to the coming of a day? As our predecessors look upon us would they shrink in our disclaiming? Would they testify to lacking wisdom as to who we became? How do we as a people forfeit all of the promise our parents knew in building our futures?

I know what my parents told me, and both are still alive, thank God, and living here in the States. Did you all know Obama's adoptive father and mother were members of the Communist party?

Mine have always been capitalists; Americans, trying to help society because it was in their best interest to do so. No, they aren't perfect, but they worked after an ideal. An ideal which was bestowed onto them from immigrant parents, who learned the English language. What the hell are we doing with ballots in multi-language and bi-lingual tax paid education systems?

Believe me, folks, the answers we need are worth all kinds of discussion, but if we forget how it was that we became who we are, then we have no wisdom to keep it as it was, and we will be less than we were. It is upon us to struggle and demand our employed and authorized to do as we see fit. A house divided is one that can never stand. Those who want us to forget the wisdom of the years, better start delivering on the bullshit of their promises. If you don't deliver, I'll shove wisdom so far up your ass that you'll seek wisdom into lifetimes of reincarnation.

How is it that nobody is demanding that the oil flow be stopped? Is it because you are so mindless that you'll accept the promises of a quasi government private industry consortium trying to impose emanate domain over an entire portion of our country inclusive of five states?

Where the hell are the environmental whackos? Where the hell is Green Peace? Are they all paids from the left? Is this the larger conspiracy of intellectuals being children? Is it like parents condemning actions of their children and then silencing them from talking about their own actions as parents? You all know how that goes right? Folks, if we want to believe we are free than we have to demand that we are in charge. And if we don't do that, than we will always have a reason to see therapists. I have fired two therapists. I am not impressed by nitwittery. Neither am I impressed by those who wish to indoctrinate me.

I try to live by the Golden Rule... I swear I do. I am more perfectly imperfect than others of my gender and that fact has gotten me in to more trouble than you can imagine. Because you are reading these words I am certainly not in jail. The problem is I am an unknown best selling author, I just don't have the whores backing the words... they just won't read the words... if they did, I would be a terrorist and in jail! What are ya gonna do?

I Convoked Hell because I was tired of hearing nitwits saying they were doing their best, when they clearly were doing what served their own interest. We as a nation are only as good as our collective determines us to be. If we want just cause, we will have it.

We sent men to the moon! We healed as no other doctor ever knew. We extended life... and for it we forgot ourselves. We became placate in the fact that we'd live forever, even while we buried those who made the promise that we could be anything we wanted.

The sin has gone so far that even our children supersede our own sense of justification. Think on this... If your child was held to accountability and you considered it wrong, what is the notion of correction? Do you threaten the thing you devised by vote?

After all you pay taxes for your school. If the school determines your kid as trouble, how do you manage that? Do you advocate for the guilty child or support the sin of giving those the authority over your child to be claimed as a problem?

And if you can figure that out, do you even get involved without threats of suing the offenders on some bullshit finding of your own desire?

Can you accept the understanding of your own vote? Somebody elected Obama!

10:31:36 PM

Okay, I understand everyone thinks I'm a hard ass. It's fine. It's been that way my whole life. To be honest, without hard asses the world wouldn't go around. Just the same, innocent minded folks would be a loss if hard asses weren't here. That being said, we have to come to a reckoning of our own morality. We have to live by man's laws, or we'll be seeing an unfriendly person dictate his or her authority.

Let me explain this because I have stood in front of judges; they aren't fun people. If you are wrong in the face of man's laws, it matters little. If you are right in man's laws but accused wrongly, well then you take the plea. Me, I ain't doing anything other than claiming guilt or walking through innocence. I will claim unrighteousness when I have accomplished being as such and there are folks you can ask about that. I keep with my spiritual leader and brother, Pastor Paol on this level...

If all of you knew him, you'd be rereading these words for your own purpose!

I guess the most important thing to carry away if you tolerated reading this far, is your own purpose as an American Citizen. A vote for representation here in the States is why folks come here, if not for nothing... THEY EARN MONEY HERE **AND send it home!** Why?

It is better here than there. What if the fucking wetbacks decided to become Americans and learn English? We'd be so far ahead than tolerating federal negligence of immigration issues of today.

That is the lie Ivy League assholes spent money on selling the New World Order. So why do we wait to receive some UN-Jesus-like ass kicking? Why do we as a country need to forget ourselves?

All right, I am an adopted child born on and in the US. I don't know my biological parents and that means little. But I am American as the forefathers wrote it; I have a birth certificate and am qualified to be a citizen. It seems a large percentage of young folks don't know what that means. Well, what that means is this: I'm old enough to be your dad or cool enough to be your professor and certainly smooth enough to be your confidant.

If I ever said these things, you should know, I am what I say. But I'd never ask to be President... You have to be crazy to want that job description. Voters who elected Clinton and Bush and Obama... Do you even know they own the elections?

Oh yes back to apathetic Americans... That is kind, because apathy works with stupid like incestuous cousins procreate. Somebody elected Obama.

7/12/2010
6:03 AM

http://www.usamutt.com/blog/blog.asp

That link is a post on my webpage, which was titled, the antichrist. Basically it is an extended bio of George Soros' life. I know who Soros is and all he is responsible for concerning the world condition. He is an evil man.

We are back from a weekend of travel. We attended a 25 year reunion for my partner, Tracy.

Then we took a roundtrip trip to the Cape so as to drop off a classmate whose family left for vacation in Dennisport on the same day of the reunion. We also took in dinner with my family who lives on the Cape, and then drove home.

In the last leg of the trip we shared scripture study; it was a nice way to prepare for offering prayer and thanks for safe passage over the weekend as we put on 500 miles in the last 48 hours.

The gathering at the reunion seemed to be a great hit at least that is what I sense. I'll know later when I update over at Facebook.

The morning is early, and unspoken conversations awoke me from my slumber with a certain urgency of a need to write. So, let me form those unspoken conversations as I can recall them for clarity of edification.

If we consider the past days of this year and we examine the research of all the links I have provided, a pattern develops. That pattern isn't easy to see, but it is there.

The only sources of information worthy of being accurate concerning the BP Oil Spill are the home grown journalists out there doing the jobs. The MSM is feeding you their canned reporting as a shroud of credibility, such as they have to do to convince those living in the folly of hypocronance that everything is going to be all right. And for doing so they can also report on Lindsay Lohan as news. Or they can focus upon World Cup championship games for the recently sold sport of soccer as a flavor to the coming international blending the NWO wants to sell.

Congress will not sign a budget and Obama writes executive orders, which violate the oath to office more prolifically than I write novels. He also distances our most closely sought allies while he invites a culture of theocracy that we have resisted for the 1,400 from its origin. We have resisted the culture because it is intolerant of a life we'd rather know as Americans or even as westerners, and the radical aspect of the culture will kill the infidels and rather gruesomely. World economies have been purposefully collapsed and the infiltration of the *shadow party* funded and built by Soros owns the DNC.

Obama nationalizes our private industries and invests money into other national ventures such as Brazilian Oil production, while he robs our national treasure to do so. This is all while the greatest manmade disaster in the history of the world continues to kill off resource in the south for greed. Profit and maintaining power through the last mechanism to stop the tyranny of our land is shackled, and that would be martial law, which could be declared for the manmade disaster to suspend the coming midterm elections.

Now you are probably thinking such a thing could never happen, but it has. This man, Soros has accomplished unthinkable and unconscionable deeds in his life as that link explains. So why would he think that destruction of natural resource would matter? Here is the trouble with that thinking; his absolute power is his own folly and thinking that he'll be able to contain damage only to the Gulf is an abomination to the creator.

Book of Genesis: 1:31

And God saw everything that he made, and behold, is was very good. And the evening and the morning were the sixth day.

For the ages of man in this world we have known our home and all of her natural bounty and mystery. It has been ours to master and thrive upon, and grow as a people. Regardless of your spiritual belief our world is a good place as it gives us everything we need to live.

Revelations 8:8-9

And the second angel sounded and as it were a great mountain burning was cast into the sea; The third part of the sea became blood; And a third part of the creatures which were in the sea, and had life died; and a third part of the ships were destroyed.

The models of this oil spill are not good. If the oil gets beyond the basin of the Gulf it will follow the Gulf Stream and it will contaminate the entire North Atlantic and maybe even the Mediterranean Sea.

Another link I think I posted spoke of a contemplation of the particular date of the explosion in context to the Jewish New Year. Was that coincidence? Maybe. Here is another thing to think about and I'd say it was for shits and giggles, but unfortunately it isn't. On December 21st, in 2012 many prophets have spoken to a time coming which describes a celestial event. The ancient Mayan Calendar spoke to the same time. Nobody really knows what will happen. It is sort of like faith, you either believe or you don't. Some say everything we know will change, if there is life it will be very different. But here is one thing I do know to be true. In our procuring resource for energy, we have forgotten our limitations or just ignored good and wise judgment.

For that negligence, we now we have something happening that has been described as a violation of all that was good in the beginning and it sure looks like what was described as the coming end. And on top of it all a possible antichrist walks among us.

I'm not gonna do morality here, that ain't my job. My job is to tell you how I see things as they are. Besides, I'll have to answer for my sins just as everyone else will. Back in the days of Convoking Hell that list of sins was many so it was a long list. We are all responsible for our condition of today and if we want to remain free we have to stop our enemies. And this midterm is the only way to get that done. Some would say force them to resign, but I don't see that happening. The Tea Party Folks are the last political weapon we have for a peaceful transfer of power back to the people and if we don't rise to knowing how our hypocronance got us here, then we deserve the hell on earth we are creating. If I am right about the arrogance of this administration our life will change for the worse. That volcano will open up in the Gulf of Mexico and the catastrophic events for it will be just like the undoing of the second angel as described in Revelations. That, my friends is just the beginning of things coming.

If we can claim back our heritage as a people blessed in the righteousness of a free people given to us in the Constitution with the guidance of being under God, we may find a path to avoiding an unwanted future. These progressive socialists in the executive and legislative bodies of our government can be fired, but it can only be done by our unified vote, which will install public servants who can't be bought by the likes of George Soros or his minions. America is the only way in which they can complete the design of their New World Order. They can't do it without America! It is utterly impossible without us.

So you see, just as God gave us choice from the Tree of Knowledge, so we have it. The question is; will we continue to be deceived in the Folly of Hypocronance by turning our backs on the importance of our choice?

I am past the outrage of indignant leaders. Anger that spurns chaotic banter serves no purpose to our need. Knowing that we are at war with those who'll claim us in our faith as being foolish or dangerous are the Goliaths that we as David's have to take down; we need not cast stones, just votes and they will fall. And we then can lead one nation Under God, indivisible with truth, justice and liberty for all.

Those who promise Utopia will never be able to deliver it through wealth redistribution. The help they have promised is unfulfilled and our condition as a country as a whole faces certain and irreparable undoing if we don't get this vote right. Obama and company have taken the will of the people to an unprecedented level of tyranny, which goes against why so many have died for keeping safe in passing the freedom to the next generation for 234 years. Some of those years we stumbled in seeing to that obligation, but during other times we have triumphed in clinging to our freedom.

Freedom isn't equality of a people. It is, rather freedom to opportunity you work as you make your reality. The purpose of governance is not to dispense charity as a function. The purpose of governance is to insure that any American has inalienable rights given to us by our Creator. People of the baby boomer age and even younger have been called "The Me Generation." If the doings of that attitude continue then what have we kept in responsibility from our parents or for our children, or even to the world we live in, the same one that is good and gives us life?

So you ask what do we do?

I offered a metaphor before to David and Goliath and there was a purpose to that and a logical purpose to be sure. Because we have invested heavily into the Military Industrial Complex it is almost impossible to reckon violence as a measure to undo the authority given to the present government. For too long they have been thinking about such a time coming. It may well come to a point in time when that is the only option left, but we aren't there yet. So we must insure that we take back our authority of Congress with those who would go to office promising to engage Constitutional measure in dismantling the executive authority otherwise known as Impeachment.

It is up to the House of Representatives to write up the Articles of Impeachment and then it is up to the senate to find guilt or innocence with two thirds of the body sitting or the President must be found guilty by the Chief Justice of the

Supreme Court. This has never happened in the history of our country. That is why some in this country think demanding resignation is the easier way to get it done. But demanding a resignation isn't the full authority guaranteed by the Constitution and only with that guarantee can we then move to hold the guilty accountable for their high crimes.

The divine inspiration written within the Constitution can be seen as David's triumph over Goliath. It must be done in accordance with what serves the Golden Rule of the living God as the Son of Man. Our stones to cast are our votes and those votes shall only be given to those who would go with the promise of seeing to the Constitutional guarantee of removing the President.

Another less likely option is to prove in a court of law that Obama isn't eligible to be President. With the resources Obama has, the likelihood of those court proceedings occurring in a period of time suitable to stop him in his tracks is very unlikely. It could fall victim to the manner in which the feds had to find Al Capone guilty of tax evasion.

One thing I have noticed since I have walked towards an inescapable growth of faith. Less people have a need to engage in discourse. It may also lead to less of a readership, which isn't in my best interest as a writer wanting to sell books. The truth of it is though I can't be worried about these things. In scripture it is said that there will be those who would wish to kill me for doing and speaking the testimony of the Living God, Jesus. It is also said that God will protect those from the persecutors of his witness and to fear not because the Holy Ghost will give wisdom of his teachings when the time for testifying presents itself.

Have you noticed our conditions as beings upon this world folks? We are at war in Afghanistan with nothing more than a promise to reduce troops by next year. Longest war in American history to date and more promises...

We are using our treasure to fund absurdity of a so-called lifestyle that turns its back on the Golden Rule by denying the first part of the rule. We are hell bent on seeing to the destruction of our oceans and freedoms are eroding. Those who deny the Glory of God grow in strength so what truly could be next?

Words leaders use words are presented in ridiculous definition as though we are all kids who don't know any better. Our ability to do as we will to make a pay has evaporated and we all suffer for the foolish notion that somehow we're not to blame for their ineptitude and criminal behavior. Our public school systems teach our kids anything other than critical thinking skills and we live in a continual orgy of hedonistic reality celebrity nitwits. Traditions of our society are dismissed as racism becomes nitwittery's defense, when the racism utilized is reversed and somehow or another every individual has the capacity to be a boss without knowing what a payroll is or even how to budget for one.

Those who have little resource expect the abundance of wanting that which resource provides and they will follow anyone willing to offer a magic pill for a cure of gluttony or lazy desperation because they seem to have invented a better mousetrap. Meanwhile the rats rule the roost and men of hypocrisy in faith rile the followers with indignation, which promotes nothing the Son of God ever spoke about in scripture. So what now? Do we continue as country hoping that these Utopian promissory nitwits will get it right? Or do we face up to being duped and get serious about what we need to do to maintain our wanted liberties?

Man's laws govern the rules of man. In the United States the founders made note of divine inspiration when writing their documents. No where else in the world has organized governance given us the freedom as we know in the States. And even as we were a nation founded in Judeo-Christian Principle our laws gave all men and women freedoms to fulfill their lives. So in the scripture when Jesus, the Living God said there would always be the poor, how is it that man thinks design of Utopia is possible? Is it by the potential of science or supported philosophical reason that we have known pride greater than our founders knew?

When the Savior and Living God speaks to harming the meekest of us all, is he not charging us with educating those who have less or even in being our brother's keeper? And if he is charging us with improving their condition as we can, what do you think he says about using them for personal position? When you promise a better living and deliver worse existence or even harm is that not sinful? What if you offer a bounty to underprivileged youth to work without proper P.P.E. for the job? Sure, you pay them, but if they get sick for the work because you didn't prepare them as to how to accomplish the compensated task do you profit in the eyes of God, or even honor his second law of the Golden Rule?

Now if you aren't of the mind to buy into faith that is fine. Personally, I don't care. Moreover I don't care if you think I am nuts for knowing my own faith, none of it matters. But you do have to ask yourself a couple of questions.

Let's take business as an example. Are you of the mind that your risk taking alone is worth walking away with huge profits from those of your stewardship and who contributed to your wealth leaving them for wages paid is a moral conclusion? Do you consider that as ethical business practice? Those who came before us found that inalienable rights were ours from the Creator and they wrote laws over time to make ethical business rewarding. Those who didn't run ethical businesses faced consequences of man's law.

What have we all seen in the last thirty or so years? Hostile mergers where CEO's who ran companies in the ground walked away with ungodly profit at the expense of those who contributed, and to what result? Divisions based upon injustice. You see, you can claim to be an atheist or agnostic, but if you burn those who contributed to your wealth, what is your reward?

Is contempt of your person for unethical deeds what you desire as a leader, or is it the end of respect? Maybe confinement or fines, even in man's law there is a measure of justice. So, are you upstanding as an atheist or wicked? Either way man's law in the States is closer than any law elsewhere in the world that is based upon the Golden Rule. That is inarguable!

And what if you are an employee? What if you use the function of unethical measure for an unwilling compensation? What if your employer is hijacked to pay unfair rates for employment, which bankrupt the concern? It matters little as either an atheist or a body of faith. Someone who knows the value of his business knows what he can pay you fairly, if you demand more than he can pay, you are unjust, because by the law of dishonoring an arrangement in God's eye you have not served in faith as a servant. This really has nothing to do with wealth or lack of wealth. This has to do with being ethical or righteous. The son of God, the living God of men is the master of all men, so if any case if servitude is forgotten, no justice can ever be rewarded in the love of life.

This is why the thinking of promised Utopia is complete and utter bullshit. When men decide that all men are equal they forget the greatest law taught by God or even the greatest law of reasoning a man can observe and that is that men aren't equal. What is equal is the ability to provide oneself with an opportunity to life, liberty and the pursuit of happiness through our Bill of Rights, otherwise known as inalienable rights. Government's duty is to see that the measure of the ability exists equally, not that it is insured. It is to promote the individual's ability to be free of government persecution according to the Constitution and in our 234 years we have refined what that means several times to be more inclusive while we come to know previous injustices. Any other observation is the lie of the progressives who want to sell socialism as a better standard of living.

I don't want to be unfair here. Just because you claim to be a person of faith, doesn't make it so. Recently the Catholic Church took its own privilege of authority and greatly abused God's favor. The abuse cases that came to be judged in man's realm of laws proved that and there are other cases of how more folks have died in the name of God. Nobody is insulated from imperfection… Nobody! Even in like minded thinking of God's brothers, we have killed each other. The horrors of lacking the Holy Spirit's wisdom are extensive and likely responsible for more death than any reason of self defense.

Having faith in my mind doesn't exclude anyone from their own choice of anything they want the choice to be. It is almost certainly opposite than that as a conclusion of me for having faith. What it means is this: if you live righteously without naming any faith I have no problems with you. The Son of Man died for our salvation and he even claimed that the unrighteous would be used in the plans of the Father. He said, use money offered by the wicked for glorifying the laws of the Father. He said, the kingdom of heaven is in the hearts of men even if they don't claim it to be. In scripture he spoke to a Pharisee and a publican worshipping. The Pharisee judged the publican in his prayer over words he used in prayer. All the while the publican made a simple prayer as a sinner without comparison based in thankfulness and repentance while glorifying God.

Jesus said, he who asked for forgiveness would be known in judgment, rather than the self righteous pretender.

I could care less if you were Muslim, Jew, Hindu, Confucius, Christian, Catholic, Orthodox

Catholic or Pagan. I don't call myself any of the dogmas. I am a servant of the Living God and then an American who lives by the teachings of Christ. Those two laws; honor thy Father as thy God and doing unto others as you would have them do unto you are my creed. As an American I have the same choices offered by God, but I am determined to live in the laws of man as I can, while observing the simplified version that Jesus Christ offered.

If I live by the Golden Rule I should be covered within the code of law that Americans rule by for civility! If I live as an American who has turned my back on the Son of Man's two laws then no judge of man can save me from an eternity he'll deny in judgment. This isn't rocket science.

Now the Living God spoke to times when the laws of men would find reason to deny authority based in presumption while forgetting the Laws of God and he said it would come with dying for a testimony of him judged as he was judged. Truth of the matter is, in my case... dying earlier for testifying would probably be more preferable...but that ain't likely to happen.

There is another thing I want to get completely straight. I think there are gospels missing from the New Testament. I think the Gospel of Mary, which is protected the Gnostics needs to be studied. My thinking is that the Council of Nicea withheld the Gospel of Mary because as first apostle to the Living God, they couldn't manage a patriarchal power base for wealth if they included her gospel.

Let me ask you something? If the Son of Man was flesh, wouldn't it reason that he'd be bound to a woman in the form of a man? And if he was, wouldn't his first confidence be to her? See, I think Jesus was all man... delivered to us as the Living God. The nitwittery of having women subjugate to man from Adam and Eve was done away with for his truth in being here. Hell, he turned water into wine. He brawled with folks. In my estimation Jesus turned a cheek to enemies as he did to those who condemned him, but to those who were just acting in their authority as men, he denied their authority over his Kingdom. In other words... he was killed for his kindness. But those Elmer Gantry types of his day... well he opened a can of whoop ass on them for denying his coming.

There is a contradiction in what most hold as a union of God and the purpose of that union. Some say women are supposed to be serving to men. I say we are supposed to serve each other to glorify God. And, if we are going to serve each other in his love... it can't be a one way load. If you are bound to a woman, as I am, without the nitwittery of man's license to marry, then you must be humbled to her in the face of your Creator. And she must honor you as the authority within the Father's love. A father's love is infinite and knows no bounds as held in the teachings of the Living God. So there must be times when the father meets a crossroad and bounces his thoughts off the woman in the Glorifying to God's love for the union. Has not the love of the Mother Mary intervened without Jesus' presence in need of God's Love?

Men and women are not equal, nor will they ever be. Same is equal. What is same about man to woman?

Well, if you are a nitwit, living in the folly of hypocronance, then I guess you see the same while you dismiss the obvious difference. The union comes from two working to glorify the gift of the Father as perfection of his love for his children rather than redefining the intent of his love. If Jesus came as a man, being born into flesh, it is my bet he was grabbing ass while he was seeing to his need as a man. Why would he present Himself as an unnatural form as a man of flesh? It makes no sense to me. Feminists like Jane Fonda and Gloria Steinham fucked the condition of women up far greater than Satan could have designed himself.

Look what we have for those stupid twits. Jesus never denied an oil job from whores, why would he deny wood polishing from a confidant or even leaving his seed behind to silently glorify the human spirit God gave man? He did say to pray in a closet, why wouldn't he grab an ass if he had the chance? I mean the whole immaculate virgin thing offers potential for his being the Messiah.

These are truths as I see them for God's truth. And when I see my country dismissing his truth of loving one another and even an enemy because it is convenient... well, my heart sinks. And while it sinks, I know that God's plan is what I serve as I perceive it. He even said as long as I was willing to glorify his love... I could get away with murder. So what gives any of these folks who turn their back on a Creator for the self serving belief in absolute power that they can wield implements of his condemnation hoping that I'd sell myself to their authority over He who has done what no other has offering a plan of duplication?

I've been trying to convince these bastards of their nitwittery in my creative blessing given to me by God and the bastards won't even consider that creative tendency, while others tell me for the read as being awesome. No, if you rest laurels without being glorifying to the Creator, I'll rebuke your authority as the warrior I am. I'm 46 years old and I have denied your self importance since I knew the ability of choice. I followed my heart in listening to the unspoken conversation of my Creator.

I see many in my country that claim righteousness of God for being Americans. I will tell you this, as an American who serves God I will rebuke those who claim God's righteousness while offering false witness, and if man's laws require so much as an American to deny God's law before being American, I'll refute the citizenship afforded to be American or at least claimed as such.

America, without being under God is no better than any shithole of a place we fought to leave in coming here for our right to life, liberty and the pursuit of happiness. And, for those Islamofacists, let me give ya a bit of advice; don't ask for my conversion, it would be easier to walk away from anything, rather than what it would take me to renounce my citizenship as an American.

Sometimes rebuking the enemy means kicking ass, and Americans used to know what ass kicking was all about when we served the Judeo-Christian following of our Founders. We just sent the Marines under the guidelines of man's law, and when they arrived they killed ya. This is what we get for listening to the progressive socialists who promise Utopia while giving away our inalienable rights to life, liberty and pursuit of happiness and while they denied glorifying the Love of God.

I am far too old to be as dedicated to a Marine's purpose, but don't underestimate what bearing false witness means to honoring thy Father as God. Before Jesus, God ordained killing of those who he thought to be displeasing in his eye. And if you deny his Son of Man as the Living God, well, shit, we go back to an eye for an eye. Marines aren't interested in equal loss... Marines are born to rebuke those in killing with finality that would come to war on a Nation under God. The second part of the Golden Rule was to do unto others... if they ain't honoring the Father as thy God.... Jesus will testify to your deeds as a people even if you killed in self defense honoring Thy Father. How is it that so many slept through the lessons and got the teacher's teachings wrong?

Oh wait, somebody elected Obama! What the hell was I thinking?

Before that, somebody else thought it would be a good idea to elect those who supported taking money from those who risked investment and applied effort to allow folks with no business of owning homes ownership of them, and elected the supporters to the congress. If you want redistribution go back to the old world.

You had two elections in coming to four years and your policies suck! Let me know how it is when you get sick in England or any other National Health Care country that puts you on a waiting list to die... then get back to me. That is if you survive the wait.

There is no other country around that can outdo America; because we do have choice above others. If you think I am wrong or you think you can do better just go to that place or buy a country and make it better. I'm sick of listening to self important idiots who think they know how to run a country for the sake of never running a concern themselves. You have no idea of what general welfare for the people means within the context of being American. The proof is right in front of your own eyes, and yet you still drag your punk ass, living in the Folly of Hypocronance ideas because nobody took the time to kick your ass as a stupid kid. They were all waxing Dr Spock's wood instead of polishing it properly!

If you never knew the Son of Man's law, God's law was what you forgot and God's Law said, *spare the rod and spoil the child*! Now for all of you happy assholes, who never thought to spank your kid when it was needed, how'd that work out for ya? Paying many lawyer bills? Or are the silly fuckers' now adult window-lickers living with you at forty years old?

Almost two years ago I wrote about this impending disaster, but I gave Obama and the liberals an opportunity to prove me wrong. I listened to your pimp dealers try to convince me of some Utopia that I was sure wasn't gonna happen. For my skepticism, I was attacked, not rebuked. I was called hateful things and even threatened. Those situations were pretty funny. My experience lends me to believe that liberal and socialist minded threats are usually only bought off instead of lived up to the giving. You bunch of cowards. It isn't like any of those nitwits earned the money. Easy come easy go.

So here we are and where the hell are all the crybabies now that the oil spill makes Katrina look like a joke? Where are all of the Constitutional protestors for Obama's illegal executive orders? Where are the protestors of illegal wars? Do you get it now? None of them have principle in it, unless there is a shakedown.

I hear leadership of the DNC claiming righteousness in the Living God's love when it serves their own justification and lesser for the GOP, not that it doesn't happen on both sides. But progressives are the violators en masse. And the *Shadow Party* is unilaterally promoting fork tongued nitwittery. What needs to be accomplished for our salvation is a complete eviction of the *den of thieves* in DC. None of them have the general welfare of the county at heart. You are all Judas' sucking up the thirty pieces of silver. And until you prove otherwise, I got a big Fuck You waiting. Any of you who made money on the backs of your constituencies don't need raise your hand, getting any unanimous vote from you vipers is impossible. If you voted for the bailouts… you need to be fired. This country needs to go back to its roots in allowing for living live based on the pretense of the Living God as Jesus without letting some asshole inmate make a tax free church for invention called kwanza, or even invite our enemies of 1,400 years to become invested.

We live under God or we begin the spiraling to punishment. You progressives take authority of man and intervene before that which gave us inalienable rights. You deny life, liberty and the Pursuit of happiness by claiming hate speech from those who would rebuke your nitwittery and then you hire thugs to intimidate those who'd be weaker and you do so with feminization of authority of the Father. The lazy pricks who wanna be men say sure; while they live with their mothers. More over they get their mothers to be mothers of their own kids because they ain't man enough to keep a woman, not without the benefit of their parents. Then you invite a codependent into your home that is gonna save the loser and she'll cope until she can't. All because Jane Fonda and Gloria Steinham told them that they could be a man. And all while your self importance bought you favor for whoever was buying.

Did you know I spoke with a friend who regularly visited Europe and the only damn thing that could be a differential between Americans and Europeans at the time was their weight? Did ya know that? Apparently fat Americans were abundant travelers to Europe until the dumb jerks elected Obama, now all the tourism comes from the Chinese to America or the employment force going to Dubai... Why? Fat, stupid Americans who need culling elected an affirmative action president. He is under the control of Soros and he worked for a guy our American citizens died in battle of freedom of a people. Yep, that cocksucker George Soros sold his own Jews out. When they were removed for genocide he confiscated the wealth left behind. Feel good now? He even admitted to the deed and you want to suck the fat pig's ass. Maybe if you had known a white Hungarian was pulling the strings and had a hand in exploiting a genocide you might have thought differently, but you were too busy window licking to do any type of research.

I gave you the analysis of how all of this happened. I did it in a book called *Hypocronance*. Those things controlled by Soros wouldn't touch it. So now I give you the evidence of your lack of faith in the American way. Your tendency to be the smartest case of Utopian treasure hunters that bought $5 maps to the treasure of just feeling good rather than working at being good and every last one of you 54% bought it hook line and sinker. A charter fisherman wishes he has such a success rate with all you dopes on every outing.

You didn't want to listen then, and I doubt you want to hear it now, but know this: If you don't live to be American Patriots under the inalienable rights of life, liberty and the pursuit of happiness, you may as well just let your teeth gnash when Judgment comes.

Americans weren't great for being communists. Americans were great because in their own mind they knew inherently to honor God the best they knew how to and to live as a free people judging only on innocence until proven guilty. All you progressives know is condemnation of the First Amendment for being there and then denying guilt, when it is presented as evidence in opposition to all your bitchin' and moaning. Hell, you don't deserve what anyone else is willing to die for because you are all a bunch of bitches. Keep having faith in Obama and company and watch everything you took for granted die.

I believe in my Creator the same as I believe in this country and this country rose to greatness and now that you silly bastards have control... earn your justice without GOD. Then try to let us know how that vote worked out for ya!

7/16/2010
2:12 PM

Yesterday the Deep Horizon Oil spill was capped; oil from the well head has been stopped. There is a window of close monitoring that has yet to be met for measuring and monitoring before they'll be sure about the success. But the oil flow has stopped. For all this good news there is some troubling news that isn't being mentioned.

In the process of fixing the well head BP employed *rovers,* small submersibles that took camera footage of the work and what else might be occurring. Evidently the original explosion sank the oil platform. The explosion produced weakening in the seabed floor and the result is oil seeping out in many different areas along with methane gas.

http://www.youtube.com/watch?v=b2RxIQP0IBU

That is a link of the feed watching the oil escape from the seafloor. The more troubling aspect of this is what can happen for the drilling BP did.

http://www.silverbearcafe.com/private/06.10/ultimate.html

That article explains a theory about methane discharges, which may be a likelihood nobody wants to think about. Some say catastrophe is inevitable. This may be one larger than any humanity has ever faced before.

The information I offered is available for those who are interested to know. Maybe those who don't want to know are more interested in more 2,000 page laws that are being called the biggest reform since the Great Depression. Maybe those folks aren't aware of life's fragile balance. Maybe they don't care about more than their own influence of power in the folly of hypocronance. It was 87 days before the well head was stopped. The legislation that has been written into law since the disaster has proven and sold to be successful and sweeping reform.

Personally, I see nothing more than continued unemployment and greater inflation. Both indicators do nothing for business investment or growth. All while the debt of government will rise to 62% of the GDP by the end of this year.

http://www.americanthinker.com/2010/07/the cbo warns the nation is an.html

Only yesterday there was another earthquake just around Washington, DC. That would be the fourth on the east coast since the Deep Water Horizon Oil Spill disaster, which happened in April of this year.

There are ten states challenging the Feds on immigrations laws today. Four states are bringing suit to the first state to impose stricter immigration laws along with the President against Arizona. A new Black Panther Party has been founded and it seems to me as though all of these things are being conspired. I spoke earlier to that evil man, George Soros. I have to be honest with you, he could pull this off. My thinking of hypocronance is well thought out and George Soros owns a big share in the MSM, he also has big money in all of the influence of industries that benefit from this type of nitwittery.

Here is where I differ from most that are lost in the frustration of the day. I see a way out. In fact, I have been mentioning that Obama would be lucky to finish his first term if he was elected. Slowly folks are beginning to see all of what I called it previously for what it is, and how the evidence proves my thinking.

I have faith in America because the divine wisdom lent to the Founding Fathers, who knew these days would come. Even though the enemy seems to have all the gravity going their way now, it is a façade. The truth of it is one which shows their legitimacy as crumbling. My proof is that Congress will not pass a budget.

What we will see is a collective thinking that will come to realize all the work of the past two years will have to be repealed. There may be criminal actions brought to the culprits of the day and usually I wouldn't care, but considering the torture delivered to ocean life; I'd have to demand prosecution of the guilty in the most severe manner.

Yes we are the masters of this planet. But if we put our own designs of materialism and absolute power above the care to that mastery, then we have lost the message of He who died to save us. Now, you don't have to believe in Christ or God. Ask yourself what your own father did for you. Didn't he put himself into the ground thinking of your benefit? Did ya have pets? Religion is real or it isn't, but what can't be denied is somebody died for you. So why would we make the earth dead for our children's legacy? Why would we give away our birthright to those who don't want to share our culture? Why would we put our youth into debt even before we could afford to give them the necessary tools to accept such a burden?

Why?

It must have been because we have turned our back on the treasures left to us. It must have been because we thought we knew better. It must have been because we can claim being great without actually having to try to prove it, because our government is going to make it a fair proposition.

Why do you think folks don't want to know the inevitable? I mean I have lived my life stating the obvious, and nobody wants to hear it...but they always come to a point that demonstrates the answer I gave... go figure? Don't they know on a day in the future their end will come?

7/19/2010
9:38 AM

This may very well be the last entry in this piece. I write today after a bit of my own nitwittery and foolishness of last night. The day yesterday was weird enough to begin as I dreamed of four folks who knocked on my door. One was a supposed census worker who wouldn't reveal an ID. There were two others; one of whom was a woman and the other was some type of security person or law enforcement authority. Lastly there was a Reverend Willie Hayes. The Reverend was not a friend. As a matter of fact, he was purely an enemy! The feeling from the dream left me knowing that someday, someone would be knocking at my door wanting to take me away.

The rest of the day was spent seeing to chores that needed doing and then the rages began. My words pained my love, Tracy even as I was hell bent on speaking them. And, for my trouble I brought a beautiful weekend to ruin in the final hours for mentioning the words which should have never been uttered.

Today I write these words with a broken finger (self inflicted) and a broken rib (also self inflicted) and I realize just how fragile life really is, not that I didn't already know it to be. And just as I am responsible for my own health... so are we as Americans responsible for our own condition as Americans.

We let our excesses become our troubles. We seem to invite the trouble for the sake of convenience and pleasure. The trouble with being American is that we as a people would rather complain about what we invited. Our childish behavior allows for the deficit of adult maturity even while we claim our destiny as our own. So many of us have forgotten the debt paid by those before us, whether they are our own countrymen or the prophets of The Son of Man as the Living God. I myself live with my transgressions; they always seem to be redeemed with a reminder not easily forgotten. For the next weeks each breath I take will be a stiff reminder of forgetting who my ultimate authority is.

We were given choice. What we do with that choice is entirely our own doing. What we realize for choices made is also our own doing. And if we continue towards repeating bad choices the only conclusion is we have is known for living by mistakes. And if we arrive at the self induced fraud of living haphazardly without knowing ourselves in truth then we do so shrugging away any love we were taught, purely for the sake of self importance above and before any responsibility of living.

Truth of most things in life is all that most don't want to hear. Those of us telling the truth know it because we live it by experience. In the end of days, nothing of this world is a carry-on piece of luggage to the afterlife. The only measure then is already known or not known in the book of life.

We create our miseries all by our own doing and none of these miseries are greater than he who paid for all of our sins combined. These are the words of a Watchman on The Gate and I will speak them to my own insanity even if it kills me.